A Trip to Doctor Woof

A play by
Vivian French

Illustrated by
Andy Rowland

Characters

**Doctor
(Dr Woof)**

Dot

**Nurse
(Nurse Ruff)**

Mum

Nip

Pip

3

Nurse: Good morning, Mrs Bark! How are you today?

Mum: Good morning, Nurse. Please can Doctor Woof take a look at Dot?

Nurse: What is the matter with Dot today?

Pip: Dot has spots – lots and lots of spots!

Nip: Yes, she's got big red spots!

Dot: Can Doctor Woof help me?

Nurse: Let's see ...

They go into Doctor Woof's room.

Doctor: Good morning, Dot. What is the matter with you?

Dot: I have lots and lots of red spots!

Doctor: Do you feel hot?

Dot: No, I am not hot.

Nip: She just feels spotty!

Pip: **Red** and spotty.

Mum: Shush, pups!

Doctor: Nurse, please get us the green bone.

Nurse: Here you are, Dot. Chew this bone.

Dot: But it's a **green** bone!

Nip: Yuck! It looks bad!

Mum: Shush! Go on, Dot. Chew it!

Dot chews the bone.

Pip: Look! Look at Dot now!

Mum: All Dot's spots are **green**!

Nurse: Oh no!

Doctor: That was my best bone for spots.

Mum: But the best bone was no good.

Doctor: Um, let me look in my book ...

Nip: That is a **big** book!

Doctor: Yes, but it cannot fix Dot's spots.

Nurse: Look in **this** book, Doctor Woof.

Dot: That book is very, very big!

Pip: I bet that book can fix Dot's spots!

Doctor: Let me see ...

Mum: Oh! Look at Doctor Woof's nose!

Dot: Doctor Woof has a spot on his nose.

Nip: Yes, it's a big red spot!

Pip: And he has a big spot on his tail too!

Nurse: Oh no! Doctor Woof has got the spots from Dot!

Doctor: Yowl!

Pip: Look, Mum! Now Dot has no spots! No red spots and no green spots.

Mum: The green bone has got rid of them!

Dot: But look at Doctor Woof!

Nip: He has lots and lots of red spots!

Nurse: Oh no! What can we do? Dot has eaten up the last green bone!

Dot: I think Doctor Woof needs to go to the doctor too!

Doctor: Yowl!